The Examined Life

James Harpur has had six poetry collections published by Carcanet and Anvil Press and is a member of Aosdána, the Irish academy of arts. He has won a number of awards for his poetry, including the Vincent Buckley Prize, a Patrick and Katherine Kavanagh Fellowship, and the UK National Poetry Competition. His books include *The White Silhouette* (2018), an *Irish Times* Book of the Year; *Angels and Harvesters* (2012), a PBS Recommendation and shortlisted for the 2013 *Irish Times* Award; and *The Dark Age* (2007), winner of the Michael Hartnett Poetry Prize. James regularly broadcasts his work on radio and gives readings and talks about poetry, inspiration and the imagination in schools and universities and at literary festivals.

www.jamesharpur.com

The Examined Life

James Harpur

TWO RIVERS PRESS

Also by Two Rivers poets

David Attwooll, *The Sound Ladder* (2015)
William Bedford, *The Dancers of Colbek* (2020)
Kate Behrens, *Man with Bombe Alaska* (2016)
Kate Behrens, *Penumbra* (2019)
Adrian Blamires & Peter Robinson (eds.), *The Arts of Peace* (2014)
Conor Carville, *English Martyrs* (2019)
David Cooke, *A Murmuration* (2015)
Terry Cree, *Fruit* (2014)
Claire Dyer, *Interference Effects* (2016)
Claire Dyer, *Yield* (2020)
John Froy, *Sandpaper & Seahorses* (2018)
Maria Teresa Horta, *Point of Honour*
    translated by Lesley Saunders (2019)
Ian House, *Nothing's Lost* (2014)
Ian House, *Just a Moment* (2020)
Rosie Jackson & Graham Burchell, *Two Girls and a Beehive* (2020)
Gill Learner, *Chill Factor* (2016)
Sue Leigh, *Chosen Hill* (2018)
Becci Louișe, *Octopus Medicine* (2017)
Mairi MacInnes, *Amazing Memories of Childhood, etc.* (2016)
Steven Matthews, *On Magnetism* (2017)
Henri Michaux, *Storms under the Skin*
    translated by Jane Draycott (2017)
René Noyau, *Earth on fire and other poems*
    translated by Gérard Noyau (2021)
James Peake, *Reaction Time of Glass* (2019)
John Pilling & Peter Robinson (eds.), *The Rilke of Ruth Speirs:*
    New Poems, Duino Elegies, Sonnets to Orpheus & Others (2015)
Peter Robinson, *The Constitutionals: A Fiction* (2019)
Peter Robinson & David Inshaw, *Bonjour Mr Inshaw* (2020)
Lesley Saunders, *Nominy-Dominy* (2018)
Jack Thacker, *Handling* (2018)
Susan Utting, *Half the Human Race* (2017)
Jean Watkins, *Precarious Lives* (2018)

By the same author

Poetry
The White Silhouette (Carcanet, 2018)
Angels and Harvesters (Anvil Press, 2012)
The Dark Age (Anvil Press Poetry, 2007)
Oracle Bones (Anvil Press Poetry, 2001)
The Monk's Dream (Anvil Press Poetry, 1996)
A Vision of Comets (Anvil Press Poetry, 1993)

Translation
Fortune's Prisoner: The Poems of Boethius's
 Consolation of Philosophy (Anvil Press Poetry, 2007)

First published in the UK in 2021 by Two Rivers Press
7 Denmark Road, Reading RG1 5PA.
www.tworiverspress.com

© James Harpur 2021

The right of the poet to be identified as the author of this work
has been asserted by him in accordance with the Copyright, Designs
and Patents Act of 1988.

All rights reserved. No part of this publication may be reproduced,
stored in or introduced into a retrieval system, or transmitted,
in any form, or by any means (electronic, mechanical, photocopying,
recording or otherwise) without the prior written permission
of the publisher.

ISBN 978-1-909747-87-6

1 2 3 4 5 6 7 8 9

Two Rivers Press is represented in the UK by Inpress Ltd
and distributed by Ingram Publisher Services UK.

Cover painting: *Cricket Game I.* by David Inshaw

Cover design by Nadja Guggi
Text design by Nadja Guggi and typeset in Janson and Parisine

Printed and bound in Great Britain by Short Run Press, Exeter

Acknowledgements

Poems from this collection have been broadcast or published or are due to be published in *Agenda*, *Fermata*, *New Humanist*, 'Poetry File' (RTÉ Lyric FM), *Poetry Ireland Review*, *Raceme*, 'Great Lives' (BBC Radio 4), *The Irish Times*, *Irish Examiner*, *The Stinging Fly*, 'Sunday Miscellany' (RTÉ Radio 1). 'Portora Royal', 'Prof', and 'The Summer World' were previously published in *The White Silhouette* (Carcanet, 2018), and many thanks to Michael Schmidt for allowing me to publish them here.

Many people have given me invaluable support and help, literary and otherwise, during the course of writing this book, in particular Ian Wild, Sarah Hamilton-Fairley, Peter Longshaw, Ania Corless, Keggie Carew, Jody Cooksley, Dick Moore and Penelope Buckley, as well as John McMonigall, who helped me financially at a time of need. I'd also like to give a special thank-you to Stephen Fry for his great kindness in writing the foreword.

A manuscript selection of this book received the 2016 Vincent Buckley Poetry Prize, and I'd like to thank the judges of the competition, as well as Kevin Brophy for his friendship in Melbourne.

Many others have read various drafts of the book and given me encouragement, advice and insights, especially Alyson, Eva, Fanny, Francesca, Grevel, John F., Lindsay, Mark, Rachel, Rosemary, and Tom. And thanks, as always, to Merrily, Patrick, Evie and Grace.

I'd also like to thank Cranleigh School for all its support, and especially pay tribute to my classmates and teachers resident between 1970 and 1975. I hope that this book has the blessing of Cranleighans past, present and future (*ex cultu robur*!).

Finally, I'd like to thank Peter Robinson, Sally Mortimore, Anne Nolan and Nadja Guggi at Two Rivers Press for their excellent midwifery.

Contents

Nostos and Doughnuts | xii
Foreword by Stephen Fry

The Examined Life

1. The Payphone Trap
Fourth Form 1970–71

    Telemachus | 4
    Scholarship Interview | 5
    Separation | 6
    Junior Dormitory: First Night | 7
    Orientation | 8
    Jonesy | 10
    The Perfect Tense | 12
    The Payphone Trap | 13
    I was Monty's Brother | 14
    Mum's First Letter | 16
    Sex Education | 17
        i. *Terra Incognita*
        ii. *Pueri*
    Hungry | 19
        i. Formal Dinner
        ii. Afternoon Tea
    Orphic | 21
    Portora Royal | 23

2. Helots
Lower Fifth 1971–72

    Middle Dormitory: Passover | 26
    Fifteen Minutes | 27
    His Father's Ghost | 28
    Fire Drill | 30
    Helots | 31
      i. Day Boys
      ii. The Matron's Tale
      iii. Cleaners
    The Master Race | 35
    The Master with the Sports Car | 36
    Still Life | 37
    Senior Study Corridor | 38
    Compline | 39
    Away Matches | 40

3. Illyria
Upper Fifth, Summer Term, 1973

    Equinox | 44
    Plato's Cave | 45
    Weekend Exeat | 46
    A Midsummer's Night | 47
    Illyria | 48
    Opera | 49
    Gatekeeper | 50
    Dance | 51
    Jubilate | 52
    Breaking Up | 53
    Holiday Sundays | 54

4. Hermit
Lower Sixth 1973–74

   Sixth Form | 58
   Senior Dormitory: Monday Morning | 59
   February 1974 | 60
   Senior Dormitory: Faust | 61
   The Housemaster's Enchanting Wife | 62
   Love Letter | 63
   Parent Meeting | 64
   School Report: Heart | 65
   Solo Squash Practice | 66
   Prof | 67
   School Report: Furies | 70

5. Ithaca
Upper Sixth 1974–75

   Taking Prayers in the Junior Dormitory | 74
   Neggers | 75
   Tuckshop | 76
   Set Text: *Philoctetes* | 77
   The Active Voice | 78
   Break Point | 79
   Lent Term Diary, 1975 | 80
   The Bricklayers' Arms | 81
   Damnatio Memoriae | 82
   Head | 83
   Angel | 84
   On Fire Watch After Suspected Arson | 86
   The Blackboard | 87
   The Night Before Exams | 88
   Examination Time | 89
   Full Stop | 90
   The Summer World | 92
   Final Report | 94
   Ithaca | 95

Nostos and Doughnuts

As someone who has inflicted upon a groaning world many squalid memories of his own childhood and schooldays, I know only too well that for many this genre – especially when it deals with a *private* 'elitist' education – is now considered firmly off limits. Closed. No more candidates need apply. I heaved at first a regretful sigh, therefore, when the manuscript of James Harpur's *The Examined Life* landed in my inbox. Decades ago, when we were students, James wrote a play that I appeared in and I have always known him to be an extraordinarily fine writer and have, in Wodehousian phrase, watched his subsequent career with considerable interest – but a school memoir? In *verse*? A *Bildungsgedicht*? Really?

Then I began to read and within two or three pages the commanding, sweetly readable flow of story, atmosphere and image immediately took hold of me and I discovered, as I think you will, that I was being borne along the current of a quite marvellous work.

Everyone reading this will have had an education of some kind or another. Few will have had one in a private school for boys and fewer still will have received a strict classical education whose traditions stretch back to the Victorian age and beyond, where names like Jowett and Porson loomed large. Yet none of this should deter or detract. You don't need to be from a family that has only recently freed its serfs to read and enjoy Chekhov, nor to have been on the run from the French police to understand *Les Misérables*. Surely we can be grown up enough to know that great writing frees us from the constraints and snobberies that surround a milieu.

The Examined Life is, perhaps like all poetry in the end, a work about memory. Memory caught in creamily assured and exquisitely compressed images (boys racing to tea, tormented by the ooze of doughnuts; the matron stiff-hipped 'in bunion-splitting shoes') and memory that evades and can't quite be caught: 'It irks me I don't remember much'. Memory, as Hesiod told us (and as Harpur knows), is the Mother of the Muses. Memories twine around images and scenes from Homer like ivy round the trunk of a tree. Inasmuch as the real meaning of 'nostalgia' is the pain and longing associated with *nostos*, the hero's return home, *The Examined Life* is a work of pure and perfect nostalgia. The poem is an Odyssey, a Ulysses shaken up in the snow-dome of *A Portrait of the Artist as a Young Man*. The scene where our hero finds out his father is leaving the family is entitled 'Telemachus' and tea with the housemaster's wife is reimagined as the Odyssey's Circe episode. For Harpur the modern world has always been best understood when seen through the lens of the ancient.

He dares to quote *Tom Brown's Schooldays* along the way, aligning himself with an ironic smile and no embarrassment to the long, now shrugged and sneered at, tradition of English public school fiction. Where Tom grows up to be a fine muscular Christian, pure and stout of heart, our hero, James Harpur, grows up to be the last scholar of Ancient Greek that his school will ever send to Oxbridge. Yet his age is the age of flares, tie-dye tees, Led Zeppelin, strikes and IRA bombs; an aching memory of the 'accidental' Gordon Hamilton-Fairley assassination comes as a terrible shock.

There is, by design, a kind of hole in the centre of the poem. Young James, our point of consciousness, is a passive and empty vessel for us to fill with our own nostalgias, our own half-remembered terrors and triumphs and so – as we do with Dylan Thomas in *Fern Hill* and John Betjeman with *Summoned By Bells* – we become the hero of the poet's memories, until he is ready to reclaim his personality. By the poem's end the elements of Irishness, Ancient Greece, prosodic flair and a restless, intelligent curiosity have indeed filled the hole and James Harpur is back in Ithaca.

© Stephen Fry 2021

For Rob ('Jonesy') and Sarah for their friendship
on the journey,
and Ian for keeping me writing about it.

The Examined Life

'You tell the truth, keep a brave and kind heart, and never listen to or say anything you wouldn't have your mother and sister hear, and you'll never feel ashamed to come home, or we to see you.'

—Thomas Hughes, from *Tom Brown's Schooldays*

'Oh no! What is this land I've come to? Will the inhabitants be violent, wild and cruel, or god-fearing and welcoming to strangers?

—Homer, *Odyssey*, Bk. 13: ll. 200–203

1. The Payphone Trap
Fourth Form 1970–71

I. Telemachus

Not long before the term began, my mum
knocked on my door. 'Can I come in?' – her voice
still practising its equilibrium.
'You know Dad's been unhappy for a while?'
I did.
      'He wants to take a break from us.
You know he loves you.'
                      I nodded –
                                her smile
too wide, her eyelids blinking out a code –
'He's moving out. But only for a bit.
He says he'll visit us the odd weekend.'
And still I couldn't grasp those eyes
leaking secrets, the tremor in her lip,
her lunging hug, all urging me to guess
that Dad had long since sailed from Ithaca;
and 'only for a bit' would mean forever.

II. Scholarship Interview

A semi-circle of unhooded eyes.
I hear the balding hawk headmaster say
'per ardua ad astra – translate it please'.
A pool of sunlight opens on the floor.
Silence. Another master pitches in:
'If you were given just a single shoe
what would you do with it? *Have fun*.
For example you could throw it high,
distract a charging bull.' They will me on
as if I were a toddler trying to stand.
'I think I'd put it in the rubbish bin.'
A sigh-withheld silence before they scratch
a saltire beside 'Imagination'.
They ask which brother I will emulate.
'Patrick.' We knew I wouldn't say *bad* John!
My first right answer, perhaps too late.
At least we're friends again. And it goes on
until they ask me if I have concerns.
I say: 'China getting the atomic bomb' –
they think this such a hoot, and I join in.

I leave and feel the onrush of relief
as if the door's unsealed a vacuum.
I breathe the summer from the South Field,
exuding every smell of childhood.
I turn and in the window the headmaster
is watching me – unthinkingly I wave,
childishly, as though he were my father –
and taken by surprise he smiles and waves
and for a moment I feel blessed
but also ... somehow sad – as if I've waved
goodbye to something not quite lost;
or which, just then, I think I've never had.

III. Separation

It's like a Sunday outing to the Downs –
a batsman's strolling out on Shamley Green
as if he thinks the summer has no end;
but then the road begins to twist like a gut
and the last bend flips us into autumn –
across a ridge the school stretches the sunset
like the Thin Red Line at Balaclava.
We drive in silence through the iron gates
and park, get out, as calm as undertakers.
I can't believe the journey's at an end
but just starting. A bell rings like fate.
We stand, talking like friends of friends
and Dad recites the pep talk he's rehearsed;
my ears can hardly bear each kindly phrase,
my eyes are turning to my bedroom posters,
and I wonder what my mum is doing now –
shelling peas while watching *Songs of Praise*?
I get a hug from Dad and watch him go;
he drives off with a grin that's not his own
and takes my childhood home.

IV. Junior Dormitory: First Night

For Peter Longshaw

The world is turning black beyond high windows.
We sit on our Crimean beds and talk
guardedly embarrassed by our new pyjamas;
Mr Macgregor comes to say a prayer
we breathe 'amen', he switches on the dark.
The clock chimes out the endless quarter hours.
Someone is tuned to Radio Caroline
and earplug-deaf intones a nasal chorus
'I hear you knocking but you can't come in'
sniggers beget sniggers, a sleeper burbles,
I want to fall to somewhere else, like Alice.
Later the moon pours in and makes things marble
and boys as peaceful as they were in wombs
lie dreamless as dogs on medieval tombs.

V. Orientation

'Avoid East House. Full of *thugs and sadists*.'
But where on earth is East
in this Escher-world of stairs ascend-
ing stairs descending stairs – at least
I'm safe inside this cubicle
compressed with Uffingham my 'shadow'
to whom I am invisible
because I'm just *too fresh* – and so
he spittles out the new-boy catechism,
his week-long task, refined to minutes.
I have five days before the prefects
will punish me for hands in pockets,
scruffy tie or cheeky grin, to learn
to make my bed with 'hospital corners'
or watch it be destroyed, to learn
the teachers' nicknames, like Neggers,
who's really Mr Richardson,
Squeak Dimmock and Vole Vallins.
I scribble Paddy Payne ('Warrior of the Skies')
and Spunky Dunky, Tojo Young,
and can't *imagine* what they look like.
I jot down classrooms – M3, R4, C1 –
and fields called Near Far Lowers
and Far Far Lowers – I'm far far gone
but Uffingham hasn't got *all bloody day*
'You'd better know the slang, *boy* …
compactum is a wardrobe
a kitchenette's a *moab*, a cubicle's a *toy*
razzer the scarlet blanket on your bed
Jacob Scratch a rugby group – *not VD*
toke and *marge* bread and butter
doof smoke, *shack* move quickly

urinal is a *pee lat, crap lat* lavatory.'
My time is up. Uffingham sneers
'Make sure you bloody learn it, *boy*'
then vanishes … for the next four years;
a compass needle spins me
to south to west to north to –
to south to west to north to

VI. Jonesy

I saw my other self at once
playing snooker in the Games Room –
head down he clucked his tongue
with every red he rifled home
or mimicked Brian Moore's crescendo
in *The Big Match* opening:
'Oh, 'gainst the post ... can he do it?
He can! *John Hollins!*'
Five years we were a gang of two
in chapel, class, assembly
or Houseroom on a winter's afternoon
all sofa-squashed and watching rugby
through the snowlight of Twickenham
on a Logie Baird TV;
or in the cosy little Music Room
falling into ecstasy
headphones electrode-clamped
slugging the Groundhogs down our ears.
Each day like hostages we dreamt
of anywhere beyond the now and here,
of unexamined lives worth living –
the mistral skies of the Côte d'Azur
a party in Weybridge, Ealing,
fare-dodging Tubes to crash a disco.
By day we watched each other's backs
at night became the other's bedtime story;
in rugby teams we were the locks
adopting Welsh accents to be scary;
and in the scrums we welded into one
as if confirming Plato's idea
that the gods split people when they're born
and make them roam across the earth
to find their other halves.

Conjoined, we roamed no farther than
the next meal, prep, assembly, class;
our future was a no-year plan.
We would've laughed if someone said
I'd be his Best Man, and me so late
for the church I felt like the bride;
that he would carry my rucksack
around the broiling Peloponnese
because I'd slipped a disk;
that I would scatter Waterloo commuters
like pigeons to clear a path for him
to make the train to Chichester –
his face the level of the window glass
reminding me again his wheelchair
had claimed him as its other half.

VII. The Perfect Tense

The bell a sizzling ECT stops dead.
Classroom doors slam shut, the train
is ready to leave and I'm marooned
in creeping quiet as if I'm going deaf
or the school's playing out a game
of sardines and I'm the last one left.

I skelter down the endless platform
but only find a deeper absence
and all I see are two contrasting doors:

one opens to a room, the glare of classmates,
a master pausing from the perfect tense;

the other to a world beyond the gates
the village road with puddles full of sky

an Austin like my mother's passing by.

VIII. The Payphone Trap

Lit up at night it lured you to the surface,
a fishing lamp mimicking the moon;
its hook baited with your mother's voice
could spin you to a world you had erased
to keep your mind in safe oblivion.

I watched a new boy squirm on it for days
his face ghoul-lit behind the quad's grey glass
gulping at the familiar; and soon
his parents turned up from his nursery past
removed him smoothly as an ambulance.

And me? Five years I never touched that phone.
But I'd picture ours ringing in the house

my mother rushing in to answer it
me hanging up, before it was too late.

IX. I was Monty's Brother

for John 'Monty' Harpur

Inter-lessons dash
an air-raid scramble –
he's parting the crush
like fire, his gang
hanging on his words,
forgetting protocol
I smile and nod
and catch him cold
but he's po-faced in time
and we keep mum:
careless emotion costs lives.
   And so I'd play dumb,
receiving hearsay –
his driving off a tank
on army open day;
fixing a third hand
to the school clock;
or drinking in the Lion,
Four Elms and Fox
at the same time.

Each night I prayed
for protection
from arrest and sadism,
each day believing in
my random luck
until one morning:
the Connaught Block,
the longest corridor
shrunk by two lads,

Jardine and Bass,
twitchy border guards
sleek-suited *SS* black –
I had no choice, breathed in
and nearly, nearly past
I looked at one –
and it was *just a glance* –
he stopped me in my tracks
You being fucking fresh?
words spat
like hoicked phlegm
he grabbed me, the other
deflating hissed *he's
Monty Harpur's brother*
I crept off – breath releas-
ing fast –
scrambling down
the Pyrenean path
to neutral Spain.

X. Mum's First Letter

At sea for days and casting memories
overboard I heard the Sirens call
and lure me to the rocks of images
of old September evenings, still golden,
when I would cycle home from school
unload my satchel, football in the garden,
rumble of a car as Dad returned late
soft-shoe shuffling the porch-lit gravel,
singing a nonsense ditty for my sake.

I blocked my ears, and tied up to a mast
of insouciance refused to unravel
before that weevilling tune, until at last
the song was drowned by distance … and the wind
being strangled in the rigging.

XI. Sex Education

i. *Terra Incognita*

Yes, I recall *De Bello Gallico*,
the morning we were parsing *scutum, hasta*,
then ... *vagina*.
                Someone sniggered. 'So!
We find that funny?' Neggers hissed.
'What word do we derive from *va-gi-na*?'

Our heads plummeted so fast they nearly hit
our desks: he picked on some poor joker
who muttered 'vagina, sir'.
                '*Correct*. Who ...
can tell me what it is?'
                No one spoke.
For unlike Gaul, Girl was still *terra
incognita*. 'Do I really have to tell you?'

He chalked up what we *longed* to know, and there
revealed at last, the mystery of woman:

'Noun singular feminine first declension.'

ii. *Pueri*

'Rest assured, I *cannot* be embarrassed.
You can ask me *anything* you want.'
She had a light-bulb of bouffant hair,
perfume as sweet as bundled honeysuckle –
and we as sensitised as monks on Athos
who smell the scent of females out at sea.
We were embarrassed, red-pocked beasts
of saurus species, voices like radio crackle
slipping octaves without warning,
and measuring manliness in jock straps.
'Ask *anything* you want' – it was like a dare.
But how could we expose our ignorance?

We scribbled, slid our papers in her box
and waited in the telegram-tension.
Fingers like forceps, she picked, and read:

'Please Miss, can you show us your tits?'

She blushed a virgin pink; we bit our lips.

XII. Hungry

i. Formal Dinner

A long low-beamed basilica
of bench-tight varnished tables;
heraldic-tinted windows
and old headmasters framed on walls
like boys whom no one's told
detention ended aeons ago.
We stand in pecking order –
House by House, row on row,
seniors at the head,
we new boys at the end
forbidden to touch our food
until we've served them.
A moment's grace before grace –
'Amen' unleashes caws
from the Rapax Legion of prefects
'Salt *up*! Butter *up*! *Now*!
'Pass the *fucking* ketch!' –
and if – for a breath – I hesitate
they'll make me fetch
all meal long, and I'll never eat
my Mulligatawny soup
or 'curried eggs Madras'
or roly-poly moulded in suet
and slapped with custard.
The hall is now a wind-tunnel
of roaring; we scamper
to and from the kitchen, hungry,
but getting even hungrier
for new boys next year –
to eat their food; taste their fear.

ii. Afternoon Tea

After the 'Harpies', *Aeneid,* Bk. 3.266 ff.

Each day the Italian cooks, Luigi, Franco,
replenished the tables of the dining hall
with crates of pudgy lumps of sugary dough
and sensed us shuffling outside the doors –
a scavenge of Harpies, schooled in grabbing:
the bolts flung back – we burst in, flocked
towards the feast, elbows flapping, grubbing
for ones that had a telltale ruddy spot.

Each day the tables groaned with buns,
each day we flew in with our filthy claws,
our lips still rank with carrion,
and left a trail of crumbs across the floor;
and memories of our foul-flowing bellies –
and Jonesy's slowly oozing grin
when he watched me stuff my cheeks so full
the head popped off
                      the spot
                                    on my chin.

XIII. Orphic

Summer evening, end of term,
strolling past the Speech Hall
I saw my brother post exams
striding out and heading for
the twilight world beyond the fence.
He gestured me to follow
and I complied in innocence
of his plans, the bushes, the hollow
from which he heaved a motorbike.
I mounted it and held his waist
as if it weren't my maiden ride;
he taxied, took off into lanes
that wove the fields with metal light
him bawling over his shoulder
I should lean sideways *with* the bike;
around the bends the road
reared up, and like oncoming cars
my fourteen years flashed by …

    The isolated Wheatsheaf somewhere
in nowhere – I slid off giddily
vibration-
brained – inside I saw beyond the bar
House Captains
enthroned in mists of thin cigars –
Elysian warriors! –
and looking round they thrust
their glassy tankards in the air
to welcome us
as if waiting all along
but always sure we'd come

as a sign of benediction.
I sat invisible and dumb
before the lager-loosened
Eleusinian secrets
faces deepening into barley moons.
    We roared back through the night
towards the North Star
this time around I didn't care
about zigzag bends or cars –
freedom threshed my hair
with joy and glory.
    Next day
I knew I'd never find that pub again.
Nor school the same
with John now gone
returning to the upper world
and I left in the Fields of Asphodel
among milling orphaned souls
looking for his shadow.

XIV. Portora Royal

We're like a troupe of travelling players
the six of us rehearsing holiday roles
as we motor through the Irish midlands
the sky blended with a layer of turf smoke.
At Enniskillen we enter Dad's old school
out-of-term deserted, a huge sepulchre,
headmaster with a warm off-duty smile
showing us our rooms in the sanatorium
then guiding us like prospective parents
to classrooms, dining hall; conjuring up
Beckett vulpine in his cricket flannels
and Oscar Wilde casting pearls to swine
while Dad slips back some forty years –
me a mere three weeks – to homesickness.
Next day a change of emptiness: Lough Erne,
headmaster's boat, glare-induced smiles
islands gliding past us on the water
Dad acting the husband without a mistress,
Mum the unsuspecting wife.
Next day sickness strikes, a tummy bug,
and it's like a scene from *Endgame*
all six of us in the sanatorium moaning
like mourners, and none of us knowing
this will be our last family holiday,
and all of us knowing.

2. Helots
Lower Fifth, 1971–72

XV. Middle Dormitory: Passover

A stationary ghost train

sometimes a boy might spring up from a nightmare
and jabber on then sink back to his coffin ...

the flashlight of the duty prefect's torch
sucked blood from every face it hit, you'd hear
a dreamer's unhinged chuckle, feral snores.

Worse was when I saw four shades appear
and tilt a bed up ninety odd degrees –
a boy-cum-mattress crumpled to the floor,
his piggy grunts converging to a cry
I panicked-prayed *dear god not me please please*

and held my breath ... then felt them pass me by

returning to the dark from which they'd crept

the corner of your sleep that never slept.

XVI. Fifteen Minutes

The first alarum marmalises sleep
and from a tent of dreams I see the siege
is just the same: Trojans look like Greeks
and the dead rise up, their eyelids glued,
stretching arms as if to break a cage.

I slipper-shuffle to the bathroom queue
and mumble the sequence of the password –
'Hurry up' 'Piss off' 'No *you* piss off'.
At camp again I fit my armoured shirt,
quiver my mind with arrows, put on greaves.

The breakfast bell sets off a cussing chaos
and the stairs cascade with coltish hooves –
I duck and weave like Paris, primed to kill,
rehearsing every boy's Achilles Heel.

XVII. His Father's Ghost

'"My son, my son! Are you really here at last?
I kept due faith – I knew your sense of duty
would keep you going on that brutal voyage –
I feel so blessed to see your face again
and talk to you and hear your lovely voice …
What distant seas and lands did you cross
to get here? What dangers did you meet?
I worried that you'd come to harm in Libya."
    Aeneas replied: "Your ghost, dear father –
I kept on seeing your poor sad ghost
who spurred me on to this twilight realm;
my ships are anchored on the Etruscan Sea.
Now father let me hold you – *don't* withdraw!"
With these words and with tears in his eyes
he tried to hug his father's neck three times …
but thrice his arms went through the ghost –
as if it were a breeze, or fleeting dream.'

I can see my fifteen-year-old self
squeezed in a cabin-lit House cubicle
and staring at *A Shorter Latin Primer*
open beside a pale-green copy book;
and like a father I want to hug him
and help him with his Virgil prep.
I know his mantra 'subject, verb, object'
and Neggers's motto 'Stick to what you know'
and will him on. I know how he feels.
It's 8.45 pm and he's so tired.
Any moment a prefect's going to shout
'Ten-to baths may go' and he and others
will leave the Junior Study Room, undress
and wallow in free-standing iron baths

and then pyjamas, prayers, bed, sleep
perchance to dream and roam the underworld
and search the Styx and Cocytus
for the shade of a father
                              in loco parentis.

XVIII. Fire Drill

The klaxon has escaped –
its pulse is pulping sleep
as if the school is in the throes
of submarine attack
and prefects burst our dreams
with shouts of 'Out! Out!' their torchbeams
rake the walls like ack-ack lights –
we scramble snatching razzers
like life-jackets
and stumble to the exit –
the wash of frosty air flings up
a spray of autumn stars –
we clatter down meccano stairs
to the ocean of the North Field
and there we huddle, lifeboat queasy,
feel naked in our thin pyjamas
dreaming through the roll-call
of being rescued, taken home to beds,
hot water bottles, mums and dads,
as the great school liner
sinks
below
the
waves.

XIX. Helots

i. Day Boys

Were like first cousins
twice removed; their eyes
soft with comforts
filled us with dismay;
they wanted camaraderie,
would hover like gnats
to hear our woven stories
of dormitory rites,
uncertain what to do –
join in or laugh
or read the signs and go
before we said piss off.
Invisible by day, at night
they lived in full
the half-forgotten life
we longed to have in school;
then back a.m. for lessons
they crept inside the gate
like missing persons
not reported absent;
they were our shadows
too close but never close
who left us every day;
who never went away.

ii. The Matron's Tale

She wore a ward-sister-white coat
    and had a tent-peg nose, curled grey hair,
    the trapdoor laugh of a marionette,
and shot out like Scylla from her lair
    to savage us about late laundry clothes.
    But during matches she was always there
to cheer us on in bunion-splitting shoes,
    bellowing across the field like a cow
    who's had its new-born calf removed.
She'd button-hole you in the corridor
    and ramble on; you'd clench your bum
    and bite your lip as every passing boy
would feel *noblesse oblige* to mime
    horrific pelvic thrusts behind her back;
    then out of the blue she would exclaim
'Long live the revolution!' to end the chat.
    One evening she invited me and Jones
    to come for cocoa in her room and watch
his actor father on her television;
    ignoring fusillades of wolf-whistles
    we traipsed along in dressing gowns
became two oleaginous angels;
    she knitted as we watched and for an hour
    we floated from the realm of timetable,
became the sons she never mothered.
    Rejoining the sniggering beds
    with tales of almost being smothered
by her bum the size of Canada,
    we drifted into sleep, smirk-faced,
    while she washed up, her faith restored
in teenage boys, the human race.

iii. Cleaners

Seemed to live in corridors.
Dog-eyed, deprived of sun,
they had, said the rumours,
escaped from 'loony bins'.
You'd turn a corner, groan
at facing one with mop in hand
as grey and static as a heron.
His eyes followed you around.

  We used to call them 'Jims',
like a species – our name
for 'almost human beings';
they always looked the same
as if they had been born
just as they were – ludicrous
to picture them as children
with mums and dads like us.

  They came to be like family
as long as it wasn't your own;
a secret everybody
pretended he didn't know;
the scrawny negatives
of scholars, rugby heroes,
blacked-out images
that popped up in the holidays
like Reggie, with his violent shakes
and face incessantly aghast
as if from shell-shock
or beatings in the past.
Or Johnny, a younger Jim,
pulling rubbery, smiley faces
and always chattering
about his mystery 'babies'.

I still see him in the corridor
observing me sheepishly,
sudding the stud-pocked floor –
I shout the ritual *'Johnnnny!'*
'You seen my babies?'
He looks so sad when I mutter *nope*
and leave him to dream of babies
and mop the grime of hope.

XX. The Master Race

We called them Nazis without thinking
and bayonetted them with nicknames.
The new Head, Van Hasselt, was Van Pin –
all *Gruppenführer* eyes and yachting tan;
and Gregson – Herbie Groin, his face
a sinister mix of beige and baby pink.
Maguire was Mugsy, who grilled excuses
as if his life somehow depended on it.
Lt Colonel Barker – Psycho –
wobbled his eyebrows when he spoke
because, they said, he'd been electrocuted.
A silvery, sly, unnerving bloke.

Nazis … until we heard the rumours that
Van Pin had got a tan on Gold Beach
assaulting the trenches of the Wehrmacht;
that Herbie Groin's face was scorched
while scrambling from a burning tank;
that Mugsy was an MI5 spy master
engaged in life-or-death interrogations;
that no-one tipped off Colonel Barker
about the delegation of teachers
from Japan, who burst into the MCR
one lazy morning in the summer …
and Psycho looked up from his *Telegraph*
and up to heaven shot his eyebrows

as he jumped through the window.

XXI. The Master with the Sports Car

A swallow left behind still lit with summer
he nested in our wintry school
and warmed us with his tales of Rive Gauche glamour,
Sorbonne in '68, Truffaut, Sartre;
his sideburns, Chelsea Boots and Romeo curls
curdled the smiles of all the war-time masters –
curriculum could never clip his wings
and we were glad he didn't stay for long
afraid he'd lose the scent of foreign things
and turn into … a teacher after all.
Better to picture him in Kentish lanes
roof down, low slung, speeding to the Channel,
to see his sunglassed eyes and mirrored glance
at poplars streaming back through wine-dark France.

XXII. Still Life

As peaceful as a soft toy, the lab rat
gave off a perfume of formaldehyde.
What fascinated me was not oesophagus
duodenum, ventricle, thyroid –
but what it was that made death *death*.
I'd never been so close to something dead.
Even just touching it seemed taboo.
What had flown its squashy little body –
rat soul, rat spirit, rat ... *élan vital*?
An incision would unflap the gory details
but would it show what made life *life*?
Pink nose, grey sheeny skin,
neat claws, exquisite tail and eyes –
it looked like someone's sleeping pet.
We murder to dissect: I took the scalpel,
braced to see the great mysterium –
yet cutting a *mammal* felt too much like
self-harming! – I pressed and sliced
and saw a pink machine without a ghost
a pointless wound
                    that will not close.

XXIII. Senior Study Corridor

You'd spy them through cracks of doors
in waistcoats, tie-less, slouched in chairs,
red light bulbs rouging posters on the walls –
a burning zeppelin, Che Guevara;
guitar riffs wafted out with rancid laughter
and the buttery smell of moab-cooked paella.

Four years I'd take to grasp this mirage,
escape the raucous souks of open-plan.
A room of my own! A hermitage,
a kettle, lamp, the privacy to measure
my life in countless instant-coffee spoons
and study … album covers at leisure;

and shut the shielding door so tight I'd spend

a slow lifetime opening it again.

XXIV. Compline

A handful of refugees from school
we've only got as far as chapel, and seek
asylum in the candle-glinted pews.

Neggers is here as well, his mouth distended
like a voracious baby starling's beak
to sing 'The day Thou gavest, Lord, has ended',

his eyes re-drifting to his Oxford choirs –
like Ovid exiled on the Black Sea coast
recalling Rome, but stuck with skin-clad tribes.

A corridor away the school is boisterous,
the House rooms jumping with electric bass.
But we are breathing in the emptiness

resigned to Sunday dying in the gloom

and Monday rising like a hunter's moon.

XXV. Away Matches

We're coming back from Hammersmith,
four teams of us, having played St Paul's;
our coach marooned at lights in Esher
the seniors start to sing and drag us into
She's got a lovely naval uniform
oh she's got a lovely naval uniform
and we're so loud that Nobby blows a gasket,
shouts us into bloody-minded cheers.
Beyond our spattered *Gastonia* bus
Esher seems so cosy, and oh so close to home!
I picture Mum pottering in the kitchen
or putting crumbs out for the birds –
and there's the red-lit Embassy Cinema
where I'd be taken for a birthday treat.
The lights change, the singing creeps up again
Oh she's got a lovely navel
got a lovely navel, *got a lovely naval uniform.*

I think of St Paul's, sleek beside the Thames,
its concrete softened by Corot trees
so different from our fields and smelly farm.
Each school we visit is a looking glass
through which we join our doppelgängers,
lank hair concealed behind the ears,
half-Windsor-knotted ties and sideburns,
speaking a pidgin of refined obscenity.
Each school is part Colditz, part film set:
Eton's a rambling Ruritanian palace
with a thousand footmen clad in tailcoats;
Worth Abbey is Agatha Christie Gothic,
its staff disguised as sandalled monks;
Christ's Hospital a Tudor pageant
with boys in knee-high yellow socks;

and Eastbourne, Brighton, Seaford, echo
with gulls – town criers calling out
the sea the sea
that make you long for holidays.

We drive through cobbled Guildford,
Shamley Green, and night is closing in.
My body's slumped, my mind's adrift
as if I've been away for years. We'll pass
the Four Elms pub then round the bend
the lit-up windows of the Connaught Block
will guide us safely into port.
Inside I'll feel the kindness of the known
in rooms and faces; assorted new boys
will bounce along to ask us if we won
like pesky younger brothers, and for a moment
the school will feel almost like home
or almost not like school.

The seniors are starting one last chorus
and Nobby's far too tired to stop us.
I find I'm joining in mechanically
Oh she's got a lovely bottom *set of teeth*

3. Illyria
Upper Fifth, Summer Term, 1973

XXVI. Equinox

Sunday evening and April light is high
    above the branchy deep-banked lanes;
    by Wonersh my stomach is at sea
and near the Four Elms the swell deepens.
    We join the long cortege of cars
    and park beside the junkyard of the kitchens.
As mum drives off I'm sad I don't care
    that much, and dart a wave like hailing a taxi.
    Inside, I climb two flights of brutal stairs
reserve two beds for me and Jonesy,
    lie back and drift into August plans
    to hitch our way to St Tropez and Nice.

I enter a state of perfect equipoise.
    It's not quite holidays and still not term;
    I'm neither man nor boy, and in a place
that's in between a school and home.
    A stillness falls like the settling of scales
    or the exquisite pause between spring and summer
when overnight the trees appear to double
    the green intensity of leaves. In limbo,
    floating from my bed to the imaginal
I flit between the boundaries of now –
    of home, of school, the south of France …

    The bell rings out: the first demonic cuckoo.

XXVII. Plato's Cave

In jackets of limestone tweed or navy blazers,
stiff-collared shirts and graphite trousers
we sat inside a cave chained up to chairs.
Our eyes were trained to stare at shadow boards
on which a stream of ghostly words appeared
and vanished, imprinting the real world.

But then one time a boy broke free and crawled
through darkness to the entrance and saw …
the 1970s! – a giant disco dance
of long-haired folk in pink crushed-velvet loons,
embroidered kaftans, bangles, platform shoes
and T-shirts dyed with cosmic swirls of turquoise.

When he returned he gabbled on and craved
the world he said he'd seen beyond the cave –
where people kissed and dressed in rainbow light.
But all we knew was grey, or black and white.
They chained him up again; we shut our eyes
and blocked our ears, and felt our teens slip by.

XXVIII. Weekend Exeat

I counted down the days until … release.
A night at home!
                    The world beyond the gates
was like a surprise party of traffic lights,
Belisha beacons, pubs.
                         Then came our lane
our drive, front door and stairs – I couldn't wait
to see my football posters once again.

But Bobby Moore looked distant; he could spot
an *adult* smile; and kissing the cup Geoff Hurst
refused to pass it on to me.
                        Each exeat
I moved away – at first polite to mum
I grew more reticent, then silent, a ghost
less haunting, than haunted by home

sweet home, oblivious of her fireside chat

counting the hours till the journey back.

XXIX. A Midsummer's Night

Me and Jonesy
are crouching in a field
like the Maquis
waiting for a parachute drop:
a scooter's whine
mosquito-loud, its engine
clucking to a stop.
Torchlight. Smith is bearing
a penitential offering:
twelve cans of pissy beer
and we absolve his day-boy sins
but only for the night.
We lie back in the wheat
our cigarette tips flitting
the dark like fireflies
and hardly move or speak
except to murmur cheers
and jump at every noise –
as if the field's concealing
a regiment of masters.
   The sky feathers to grey
and sudden as a cockcrow
the school clock chimes the hour
several fields away.
We say goodbye to Smith
sneak across the border
tiptoe through the House
past guardrooms of prefects
rejoin our stiffened beds
and drift to whisperings of wheat
in a field that's yet to lose
the crushed-down dream
of our three body shapes.

XXX. Illyria

(*Twelfth Night*, Regent's Park Outdoor Theatre, June 1973)

'What country, friends, is this?'
'Illyria.' We're shipwrecked in Illyria
and me and Jones are poised to flee
across the border to the *city* ...
a black-out catapults us from our seats –
like actors darting from the stage
we dash to find the exit of the park
and brief asylum in a pub
but the more we charge around the more
the park's a seamless circle –
the only thing escaping is time –
we have to scale the railinged fence
and Jones succeeds but when I try
a spike pierces my leather sole
as though it's just a layer of skin
and Jonesy laughs as if I'm Feste
larking around, he shouts 'Jump!
For god's sake, jump!' but I'm impaled –
the world outside's a leap away
the inside world an iron quill
that etches lines I know too well:
'What country, friends, is this?'
'School. You cannot leave. It's school.'

XXXI. Opera

for Hilary Davan Wetton

Curtain up, the music master's car,
a backdrop of the silhouetted school;
blackout, then
                a twinkling village
suburbs of promiscuous orange lamps
the West End's glitz and Covent Garden
   glowing like the Parthenon.

Scene change, Crush Bar hubbub
champagne chandeliers silver-slippered women
contralto laughter
                in seats of crimson
we watch mad Wozzeck stab his lover
and turn the starlit forest pond incarnadine
   by throwing in his bloody knife.

Lights off, when they come on once more
it's midnight at a wood near Shere
the master stops and leads us up a hill
to gaze at the full moon
                the whole of Surrey
unrolls in tops of trees so still
   a song would reach the English Channel.

The final act, now back in school
we're creeping in the dorm; I lie in bed
and close my eyes and there, the moon again
like a spotlight
              I bask and bow in the applause
that sweeps me off the stage beyond the world
   beyond the falling curtain.

XXXII. Gatekeeper

On stage I watch the pilgrims and Hassan
advance towards the gate. I shout
'Ho, travellers, I open. For what land
leave you the dim-moon city of delight?'

Each night I say the same, each night they go.
I lock the gate, then open up my own
invisible to the audience – for though
it looks as if I'm standing there alone

lights dimmed, curtain poised to drop,
I've left the stage, the school, the village and
I'm following the pilgrims' footsteps
along the golden road to Samarkand.

XXXIII. Dance

A minibus with Nobby driving,
ex-army gym instructor, and we
a dozen, spotty sultans dreaming
of Prior's Field's seraglio.
We shout out favourite types of girl
like bidding at an auction
until Tate, sweet natured, oafish, gibbers
'I'll never get one'
and wipes his thick-lens glasses.

   A prim mistress leads us to a hall
where *real live girls* in party dresses
with swirly eyes inspect us all
like cases on an airport carousel –
I lunge at one – she acquiesces
and my relief is clearly hers as well:
we grin like village idiots
shouting above the disco noise –
I feel the pressure of an O Level
to crack a joke with every phrase
and grade myself by every giggle;
and when we cannot bear the clash
of simultaneous splutterings
we dance and in the heated crush
I turn … and see two visions:
the glow of Tate's seraphic face
as he stuns a brunette with his bopping
then struts as Jumping Jack Flash,
his loosened waistcoat flapping;
and … *Our Nobby of Gymnasium*
his sculpted bum in skin-tight jeans,
no longer bodyguard but Bacchus –
his clean-cut National Service grin
a beatific ooze of sex

as he boogies with the mistress to T-Rex.

XXXIV. Jubilate

We wish the chapel bell would just sod off.
But it takes its toll, coercing us to pews
of niggly nudges whispers wheezy coughs.

The masters come and turn us into stone,
filing as slow as mourners, two by two,
and pious as Pardoners in long black gowns.

The organist cuts his gothic-horror chords.

Silence; murmbling rotes of prayers;
a psalm meanders; we fight to stitch up yawns
as the preacher scatters pearls to swine.

Then Stanford's *Jubilate* shakes the air:
we sing like lions, a pride of one
primeval roar – five hundred gentlemen

like chanting Millwall skinheads at the Den.

XXXV. Breaking Up

I sit on my trunk outside and watch
the school disgorging boys from every door.
My beaming mum arrives an hour late
and I'm so frantic to rejoin the world
the journey back seems longer than the term.
We stop for petrol, stop for food …
and then a garden centre.
                                    Home at last
I put on scruffy clothes and look for clues
of my old life, like Odysseus in his palace
disguised as a beggar, feeling his way
and entering a world of déjà vus:
a frayed carpet, gilt mirror, battered sofa,
the dangling threads of mum's embroidery,
still unfinished; and no suitor to be seen.

XXXVI. Holiday Sundays

I'd hear the gravel crunch beneath Dad's car
and watch him tennis-stiff approach the door

white shorts below the belly line, knee strapped
and brylcreemed strings of hair across his scalp.

Inside, my mum would kiss his bronzed cheek
as if he'd just come back from work

three years ago; he'd ask me how I was
but when I spoke the interest left his eyes

and let my words wither on the vine.
The silence lengthened after he had gone.

It felt as if it wasn't Dad who'd seen us
but some amnesiac returning to the house

to gather clues about his previous life
dismayed he hadn't found his son and wife

but two strangers studying his face
as if perhaps they'd known him in the past.

4. Hermit

Lower Sixth 1973–74

XXXVII. Sixth Form

'Now is the time in all your lives, probably,
when you [sixth-formers] may have more
wide influence for good or evil on the society
you live in than you ever can have again.'
—from *Tom Brown's Schooldays*

Among fire escapes and kitchen bins
I feel like a prince among the new boys;
or a priest absolving their parents
as they perform their ritual goodbyes
and amble to their getaway cars –
as mindfully as tightrope-walkers.
Sixth Form. A sixth-former at last!
I clamber up to find the Senior Dorm
and flop on a bed. It's so luxurious here –
just ten of us, the bathroom right next door.
Lads arrive with gilded hair and tans
to rage against the dying of the summer.

Evening gathers in the windows
and drifts as slow as pollen to the floor;
between the bantering and wolfish smiles –
Harpur's going to be a vicar!
Hey lads, he's Neggers's love child! –
falls the shadow of Plato, Virgil, Luke,
two years of ancient studies by myself;
the flicked-on lights flick off our jokes
and wash the window glass with darkness …

The bell shreds us like an exorcist's shout –

the ghost of summer shrieks, flies out.

XXXVIII. Senior Dormitory: Monday Morning

It's icy. I'm snug in bed aware that Jones
is crouching down and whispering in my ear,
suspiciously benign: 'You awake, James?
You'll never guess – I've got you out of Latin,
I've settled it with Neggers, you're in the clear.'
He knows how much I'm dying to believe him;
I dread that class and now he's seized his chance:
'Relax, I'll run your bath and get hot towels …'
I close my eyes. I'm gone. And he's relentless:
'But first I'll bring the croissants, café au lait,
and then perhaps a fat hand-rolled *Gauloise*?'
I dream of sky-blue France, of St Tropez
and float in heaven … till I hear the bell
and Jonesy's chuckle fading into hell.

XXXIX. February 1974

The sky has given up the sun for Lent.
Bombs, three-day weeks and strikes
are rumours till the nightly power-cut
and school is flashlit into mineshafts
or the Underground in the Blitz.
The sky has given up the sun for Lent.
Each day's a cold war, a day of waiting
for the power cut, for a switch flicked –
it's hard to concentrate in lessons
or on hockey pitches stretching like Siberia;
or in the tuckshop where we debate
between asphyxiation by socks
or hypothermia from open windows.
The sky has given up the sun for Lent,
it's like a siege or war of nerves –
impending 'mocks' and the apocalypse
each night – the power-cut
is like a nuclear winter – under pillows
transistor radios crackle news
from Luxembourg or pirate ships
resisting the slaughter of the North Sea:
coal's running out, wildcat strikes
are multiplying, the world might shut
down with one last power-

XL. Senior Dormitory: Faust

One time a silhouette materialised
from nowhere, sat on Brewer's bed, dead quiet.

His nimble fingers quick as two white mice
flicked lit matches at the pillowed hair,
sparking a dread – and hope – it would ignite.

We were transfixed by every little flare's
trajectory, the sudden chiaroscuro,

as if we'd fallen into Rembrandt's *Night Watch*.

But we did nothing to arrest the shadow

our souls becoming mephistophelean
we felt our wills dissolve with every match
and could not, would not, intervene

not even when a cry roared out like flame
above our laughter, though not our whispering shame.

XLI. The Housemaster's Enchanting Wife

After 'Circe', Homer, *Odyssey*, Book 10, ll. 229–243

We shouted out for her till we were hoarse.
Finally she opened up her gleaming doors
and invited us to enter. Still unsuspecting
we ventured in – except Eurylochus
who smelled a rat and stayed outside.
She welcomed us and sat us down on chairs
and couches, served a fragrant brew of wine,
barley meal, honey … and a pernicious drug
to make us utterly forget our homes.
We drank it. She tapped us with her wand
and turned us into pigs then penned us up.
There we were! Grunting hogs with bristly hides,
our minds intact, as human as before.
Trapped in sties, we wept. She threw us acorns,
beech nuts and cornel berries – the sort of food
pigs dream about when wallowing in mud.

XLII. Love Letter

All day it lies unopened in my jacket.

The envelope, inviolate and suspenseful,
protects me like a cigarette case or locket
a girl might give her sweetheart off to war.

It charms the hours; I feel invulnerable
to verbal bullets shrapnel mortar fire
flying around the trenches of the school.

Sometimes unwatched I take it out and crave
to read the curvy female majuscule …

but wait till night: alone I chance my luck

and slit it, count the x's, feel her love

illuminate my face – as if I've struck

a match and tensed a hundred snipers' hands

on the darker side of no-man's-land.

XLIII. Parent Meeting

i.m. Stephen Winkley

Outside the Doric Speech Hall
headlights die, a car door opens
and Dad waves wildly, calls me
like a new boy spotting his parents.
He seems shorter, more stout –
we skim a hug and go inside
his clubland bonhomie bubbling out
all over Dr Winkley, who's wry
and scholarly, mutely amused
to see the block I've been chipped from.
I want Dad alone. I want his news.
I want to tell him how I am –
but they collude till I'm invisible
and weigh me on some scales
and finally conclude: 'Oxbridge Material',
as if I'm just a bolt of wool.
The die is cast.
And Dad's so chuffed
that when Winkley says *Of course
he'll have to work his socks off*
he guffaws as if it's the best joke
he's ever heard.
　　　　　　　He leaves at once.
I watch his headlights blaze the road
until the bend, and then he's gone
my *pater ex machina*
dropping facial tics
of unsaid words like litter
at a picnic.

XLIV. School Report: Heart

The white cover of my report is calm
and quiet; but when I open it I hear
the scratch scratch of tiny gold beaks.

Winkley: He will be fine, if he doesn't get too lonely.
Bain: It's hard to generate momentum in a set of one.
Vallins: I've been concerned that his existence
             has become so largely that of a hermit …
Van Hasselt: He does not wear his heart on his sleeve.
             But then why should he?

Those are *their* reports, and this is mine:
It's strange how suddenly it's occurred –
that after three years of enforced joining in,
he has withdrawn himself to guard
his spirit, heart or sanity. It's clear
he can no longer bear communal life;
no longer of the open cubicle world,
studying subjects no one wants to share,
withdrawn from teams he used to play in,
he's bunkered in a cell, his brain feeding
on words extinct in medieval times.
His heart is shrinking from his sleeve,
his friends are folk like Oedipus, Cassandra.
Oxbridge is his Troy
and he will sacrifice his Iphigeneia
to get the winds to blow him there.

XLV. Solo Squash Practice

Relief! this sanctuary of emptiness

Shinto wooden floor   plain white walls

almost-secret door   the ceiling's glass

Mondrian stripe of red across the plaster

the way the angles trick and tease the ball.

I build up heat a rhythm faster   faster –
with every smash the whirl of rowdy space
and glare of open toilets voyeur baths
diminish into a state of grace –
the ball returning metronomically
transforms the twitchy bell-tormented self
to reflex
          and the glow
of mindless body

each rifled forehand gathers points of stillness

each slapping echo rings in silence
                        silence

XLVI. Prof

i.m. Professor Gordon Hamilton-Fairley (1930–1975)

At home that autumn morning
I heard the radio blur …
'a car bomb … no warning
Campden Hill Square
man dead … device set off
by his dog' … *please God
don't let it be the Prof.*

I used to wonder what
on earth he thought of me,
his daughter's boyfriend
arriving late post-party
toothbrush stuffed in denims
squiffy, slurring words.
Yet he was always gracious
although he'd been on wards
all week staring at death;
or conducting seminars
on lymphomas, leukaemia;
or lowering the blood pressure
of staff at St Bartholomew's.
I felt as if I'd lost a dad
again – the listener
I'd never really had;
a soulful empathiser.

I can see him at their cottage
light fading as he pokes
a hedge to find a guinea pig
and save it from the fox;
nineteen-fifties retro
side-parted auburn hair,

an open face, crooked elbow,
attentive, ready to share
the countdown of his days;
for we had no idea
that he, a cancer specialist,
was fighting cancer too.

'Death of a Life Saver'
the headlines said. The bomb
was planted for a neighbour
delayed from leaving home.
Fate had dealt its cards
and simply waited: windows
imploded; from the body parts
they identified his elbow.
I went to Holland Park
and joined the family
delirious with shock
crying, laughing, alternately;
that night the four of them
slept together in one bed,
a tangled heap of limbs
like the raft of the *Medusa*.

The evening of the service
Mum and I met Dad
in his Fleet Street office,
the two of them re-glued
for just an hour or so –
and it was like the old days
them dressing up to go
to a West End premiere.
Dad asked about my tie
and looked a little miffed
when I replied

that it had been the Prof's.
We headed for St Paul's
the sky gunpowder grey
Dad musing on the war
when bombs were two a penny.
We thought a hundred souls
would come, but thousands
filled the floodlit cupola:
it was as if all London
was in mourning, the dome
rising like a huge balloon
on a myriad candle flames
and breath of hymns.
Afterwards we went back home:
Dad to his second wife
me to my single Mum;
the Prof's four children to a life
without their Dad.

In the cathedral crypt
Dear Prof, your plaque
declares in stone that it
*matters not how a man dies
but how he lives*:
a bomb may vaporise us
but cannot even bruise
the memories of gestures
and acts of mercy or malice
that stamp us thereafter.
Like placing a device
beneath a vehicle;
or saving a guinea pig
while Fate like a fox
is waiting in a field.

XLVII. School Report: Furies

Eyes closed I see the Furies creep towards me
in tragic masks and form a semi-circle.
Three step forward out of line and hiss:

Winkley: He *must* devote three weeks of holidays
to get to grips with Greek translation.
Bain: He *should* read Herodotus
and *The Persians*. Anything else is a bonus.
Neggers: He *must* make himself more acquainted
with Greek oratory and tragedy.

I open my eyes and blink the Furies away
   from Cannes beach, dismissing the Oracle:
   'Harpur, you'll probably be the last boy
at this school to take Greek A Level.
   A hundred years may die with you.' It's not that
   I'm not dismayed my trusty old *Liddell*
will moulder in the library; and it's great
   deciphering Plato and Euripides
   and probing the Victorian brains of Jowett
and Jebb ... but the crush of sand and sea,
   the topless women and *le sandwich* sellers
   obliterate Greek particles and the *Odyssey* ...
until sunset, when the Furies stamp my *moira*
   across the darkening atmosphere –
   their spangled giants striding through the stars:
Andromeda, Perseus, Cassiopeia.

5. Ithaca

Upper Sixth 1974–75

XLVIII. Taking Prayers in the Junior Dormitory

Angelic in their new pyjamas
they look at me as if I were their dad.

My last is like my first September
the skittish laughs of stuffed-down dread
the sense of vastness in the eyes

I turn the lights off after their 'amen' –

the darkness blots the rows of horrid pupae
I cannot wait to never see again.

XLIX. Neggers

i.m. Christopher Richardson

A bah-humbug pout of indigestion
on his razor-rashed cherub face,
his hair a golden fleece, a little tarnished,
he went to sleep in Rome, woke up in Troy
and we would sit like Romulus and Remus
in a room designed for thirty boys
endure each other's moods and cabin fever.
He skippered me through the *Odyssey*
each line a wave that led to Ithaca.
I had no friend to help me in extremis,
nowhere to hide, and felt his melancholy
that his Oxford First had come to this:
one pupil, grades-obsessed but unwholehearted,
willing the lesson to end … before it started.

L. Tuckshop

'They wished to stay with the lotus-eating people,
feeding on lotus, and to forget returning home.'
—*Odyssey* Bk. 9, ll. 96–97

Like long iced buns the neon strips
darken the flakes of snow beyond the window.
I sit with Quilter, Kennaway, Jones
on slouch-inducing benches, sipping tea.

Between silence and crackle of crisps
we drop non-sequiturs that get the grunts
they barely merit; the pale formica top
resists the imprints of our elbows.

This is our safe house, our Speak Easy.
The only adults are the village women
sleeves rolled up dispensing motherhood
endearingly innocent of our exams.

Each shush of steam the metal urns release
dissolves my mania to seek and learn
the magic word that might just save the day
in the unseen translation paper.

My eyelids grow heavy in the warmth
my stomach muscles remember how to soften:
I want to stay forever with the Crisp Eaters,
keep munching crisps, munching crisps.

LI. Set Text: *Philoctetes*

At first he seemed too pitiful – marooned
on Lemnos by his shipmates bound for Troy
who could not bear his stinking gangrene;

but I grew fond of him and he of me,
I read at night, he hunted food by day,
two loners glad to have some company.

Then Neoptolemus arrived out of the blue
with honeyed words and claims they needed him
at Troy after all – but he refused to go

and howled *I want to see my father, my home*.
Worn down, confused he left our 'sea-lashed island'
to join the bloody war. I stayed, alone,

dreaming of him and Troy, the world beyond,

and a small white sail
                        breaking the horizon

LII. The Active Voice

The school is hushed, asleep. I'm wide awake
my lamp as bright as Artemis's moon
above a sea of open books, all Greek.

The voice is nagging me *You need an 'A'*:
revise another verb   I'm slowing down
but conjugate 'I work', *ergazomai*

and do the aorist of *phroneo* 'I think'

Go on, one more my yawn's a silent bellow
for help, the tenses are a labyrinth

exams are closing in but I will never close
the gap of ignorance, like Zeno's arrow.

One more might make the difference   my eyes
are pink with fear of failure   *Don't go to bed.*

Alright, just one… *phobein, phoboumai* 'dread'.

LIII. Break Point

The squash ball's stinging hot, the court
as sweaty as a hammam
but I'm so cold
this Dulwich number one is slow
I should be beating him –
thrashing the ball like driving Satan out but out
it goes or smacks the tin –
the master in the gallery shrieks
come on come on – *piss off piss off*!
my lungs are shot – must stop
must shake his hand ... I mustn't shake.

The minibus is an ambulance.

The doctor mumbles 'Glandular fever ...
you're going home, the only thing is rest' –
'Can't do that sir, got grades to get'.
I enunciate as if he's thick or deaf.
Two As and a B. Like blood groups. I protest
I can't leave school
but know I have to stop my will
from smashing gerunds round
the echo chamber of my brain
all day and through the night until
the snatch of sleep ... until
the bell begins the match again.

LIV. Lent Term Diary, 1975

Dormitory, my room at home;
playing fields, a patch of lawn;
school assembly, me and mum.
Gas fire purrs; like a cat I yawn
and stretch in bed, glands raised,
numbing to the drone of Radio One.
I read the *Odyssey* but drowse
like Elpenor before he plunges
doomwards from Circe's roof.
We meet at meals, swap words
like ceremonial gifts then off
I slouch towards my mangled bed.
Winter hardens around us.
Dad arrives one Sunday morning
to say hello, inspect the gutters
and tut about the antique heating.
He tells mum to sell the house.
My schoolmates send me cheery letters
perhaps an exercise in class?
Their scrawl is strangely intimate –
I can't believe I'm schoolsick.
Each day my purpose breaks
a little more, Oxbridge is sinking
and draws me into a vortex
of regret, sadness then relief
as a drowner swallows water, then peace.

LV. The Bricklayers' Arms

Magnolia light of late April
descends on bobtails on the hedges
by Shamley Green's bus shelter;
as hesitant as Lazarus edging
towards dazzle and bird roar
I enter the pub that's full of pals
en route to school – they turn and cheer
as if I'm a lifer sprung from jail,
and yet I've only missed a term:
there's Jonesy poised to throw his darts,
Dick Moore with his Adonis curls,
Phil Deeker in his Easy Rider shades.
I sip my pint of Bass, salute
my glad captains … and taste the grief
that soon we'll be at home for good
and filing into
                the orphanage of life.

LVI. *Damnatio Memoriae*

The South Field freshly cut
wafts in the summer a final time;
the tennis nets have been winched up,
the cricket pitches freshly lined;
the swimming pool, unpeeled,
exudes a calm caerulean blue;
and hedges thicken the boundaries
as if they know we plan to flee.
Our lives are like the fate of leaves –
the wind scatters them in autumn
but then once more in spring the trees
bring forth another generation …
Already I can picture strangers
preparing to initialise
our desks and empty lockers,
scratch names from books; for a while
Mnemosyné herself may save us –
the Years below us might perhaps
retain our fading images
like sun-bleached holiday snaps –
until they too are swept away
and we all become one flitter-haze
of bats in Hades oblivious
of new boys oblivious of us.

LVII. Head

Examination pressure's been turned off.
The only As and B I care about
are chords I strum on my guitar.
My study's like a fortune-teller's tent –
red light bulb, killims on the walls,
and I can read my future for the term:
a time of winding down and tennis
a time of soft revising, decent grades.
Knock knock. Only masters knock!
I grab a Latin dictionary and shout
'Come in.' Door opens. God. Van Hasselt.
Squire-like in his three-piece herringbone.
He's clutching his lapel, means business,
and perches stiff-relaxed on my bed.
'I hate you James.' *What does he mean?*
'Don't do that sir, it isn't good for you.'
'Good answer!' He's brought Smile along.
'I hear you've given up on Oxbridge?'
'That's right, sir. Never get the grades.'
Smile hides. He looks away, turns back,
his irises the blue of Royal Delft.
'Won't do, you know. School needs you.
Parents will be proud of you. They will.
Don't let us down.' Smile peeps out
devoid of anything a smile should have.
A blush of silence; he nods and leaves –
the door is like a whoosh inside my head
as if he were a plumber who's done
his job, and turned the mains back on.

LVIII. Angel

After another cranked-up day
of Tacitus's cynicism
of reading a letter not from Sarah
but Paul to the Ephesians
I light up late at night, puff
a wobbly ring of Saturn
across a crowded study
and quoit it onto Codrai's finger.
This attic room in West
feels safe, a corner of the cosmos
that masters never penetrate;
A Levels vanish in riffs
of 'Starman' and clouds of smoke.
Knock knock.
It's like a knock-knock joke –
but the punchline's Penguin Clark
who peers around the door;
glowing like meteorites
our fags hurtle to the floor.
Expulsion awaits.

Next morning I obsess
at footsteps accelerating
past my room as if they've guessed
I'm just a dead man waiting.
And then at last a slower tread.
Knock knock. I know the punchline.
Goon enters, sits on my bed
as if he were a prison chaplain
his horsey leathery face
ingrained with cricketer's tan
is doubtful – as if he's poised
to give an LBW decision.

His words could finish my career.
My life. But he declares 'Not out!'
and talks exams, youthful errors,
but I am floating high and nearly shout
that I – yes *I* – am un-ex-pellable
a sacred life form, holy, holy, holy,
an *Oxbridge angel*!

trailing clouds of glory.

LIX. On Fire Watch after Suspected Arson

Past midnight and the school is quiet
except for footsteps – vigilante prefects
shining torches into startled interiors
of boiler rooms, cupboards, backstairs.
I case the library, and then clock
I'm by the Head's study. The door's unlocked.
I enter, strafe the room with light
and at the window see the spot outside
where years ago I waved at Mr Emms.
I sit down, put my feet up on the desk
and flash-recall my scholars' interview
and what I'd do with a single shoe,
the pricklings of interrogated shyness.
Now I know *per ardua ad astra* means
by struggle we can reach the stars
if not A Level grades. From there to now
my past is like an unlit bonfire crammed
inside my head. Then in the window frame
I see the arsonist! He waves – I wave –
then both of us take out a match
to turn my memory school to ash.

LX. The Blackboard

Is like my mind before examinations –
as if the very words I need to know
are trying to hide in corners – ghosts
of hieroglyphs from previous lessons
quotes and formulae not quite erased;
they tantalise me as I reach for them –
as if they know I'm running out of time
with darkness just a single wipe away.

LXI. The Night Before Exams

My study is a refuge
of monkish reading, then
The Dark Side of the Moon
croons through the air
from windows opened wide
around the Quad
to let the balm of summer in;
and I revise my worries
fretting by rote
and envious of the English set
tucked away in studies
testing one another
giggly-high on coffee.
I'd sacrifice a goat
to make the gods divulge
which bits of the *Antigone*
will come up; instead
I microdot my notes
to chemical formulae.
    The clock strikes one.
Electrically awake
I snuff my bedside light
and see scintillas of fear;
then feel them come –
the daughters of the night:
Clotho spinning the thread of fate
Lachesis measuring it
Atropos with her 'abhorréd shears'.

LXII. Examination Time

The hall's as still as a Dutch interior:
Neatness and order; desks within a grid.
The sun has cast gold rhomboids on the floor
and small white sheets of paper lie in wait.

You sit and check your pen, then hear the word
and plunge towards your unturned-over fate

and find a subaquatic silence: time

goes out the window merging with the summer

faint footsteps   voices   bells like tinkling chimes …

From far away you hear 'put down your pens'

and see a miracle's occurred: your papers
are filled with words that someone else has written.

You rise and watch the world speed up again
and step out from the canvas of the painting.

LXIII. Full Stop

A classroom three floors up –
I pray to Mark to help me write on Paul.
The last exam, and the white paper
is dangerously restful …
Raymondo the invigilator
is young, soft bearded, browsing a book
as if in bed about to turn his light off.
Outside, the school's demob euphoric –
the thump thump of bass guitars
are lung-collapsing trumpets at Jericho.
I herd my thoughts towards Paul
the clock hand shifts like a nervous tic
a loss of focus could scupper
my life for years, perhaps forever;
so when I hear Rob Curling calling up
and mimicking a girl we know
like Romeo and Juliet in reverse
I curse and pray to Mark *and* Paul.
Again the clock hand shifts
and this time it's a starting pistol –
I scribble out a scrawl of ink
as madly as the Gadarene demoniac –
my thoughts are legion and I fear my Greek
will look like squiffy Arabic.
I glimpse Raymondo looking up:
'A minute left,' he growls
as if it's life he's speaking of.
      Full Stop.
My last full stop at school.
The breath that I exhale
feels like the first one in five years.
I gaze outside and see the flagpole
a boy standing there

raising a flag as if to toast
the last stage of my journey.
I wait to watch the school's crest
unfold itself in gold and blue;
it rises higher, flick flick flickers
catches the breeze and flutters
into a pair
           of lacy black knickers.

LXIV. The Summer World

For Rob

It irks me I don't remember much
about the days between the last exam
and the end. Did we party, or slouch
towards that unbearable freedom?
Weren't there rumours and plots?
Smuggling a sheep into Herbie's study,
streaking at supper, an alarm clock
primed to go off during Speech Day?
So I ring you, ahead of our weekly ritual,
tightening my grip on the receiver
until the click, sound of a shuffle,
TV blaring, whirr of your wheelchair.
We sound like beret-wearing veterans
forgetting we've spoken the week before,
eager to re-live anything we can.
I guide us, gently, to our final summer
and hear your brain working hard
as if you're in the middle of French Oral.
Eventually you say: 'I was feeling good.
The last exam – History? – went well.
It was a long hot summer, wasn't it?
I remember walking by Gatley's Pond
and stopping, feeling at ease … that's right –
I heard youngsters in the swimming pool.
It was so hot I'd taken off my shirt,
wearing just my corduroy waistcoat.
I can't remember where I'd come from …
or where I had to go …
just the heat, laughter and happy shouts …
And then there was the first eleven,
my final match – fifteen not out! –

the shock of mum arriving with a wig on.
Wigs were really awful at that time.
They never told me she was so ill
they didn't want to ruin my exams.
She died the day before my results.
Three As. That morning ... I didn't know what ...'
You stop-start to the end of the sentence
but your words are merely sounds
for I have drifted back to school
the sunny path beside the pond
and there you are weightless and peaceful
listening to the laughter of children
happy and invisible.

LXV. Final Report

It's like I've stumbled into someone's funeral,
mourners whispering to each other
around the flowered coffin in the graveyard.

Barlow: Undoubtedly it was hard for him
                to make up all that lost ground …
Megahey: The break in continuity went deeper
                than I thought …
Neggers: I was alarmed to find how far his absence
                had affected his development.
Corran: One hopes that he will gain the grades …
                I fear his illness has set him back too much.

I close the report, like a lid, to shut their voices out.
But the mourners stay whispering …
                                      becoming less distinct
as if they're walking away or I
                          am inching down
  into the darkness
                of another life.

LXVI. Ithaca

The chapel roars 'Jerusalem'
me and Jonesy side by side
for one last time. At 'Let us pray'
we close our eyes, bow heads
as if about to lay them on the block.
I picture what will happen next:
we'll heave our coffin-heavy trunks
to open boots and say goodbye
as if we'll all be back on Monday;
then drive off through the gates to join
the vast unbridled summer
lines of roadside trees and hedges
flittering silvery leaves
as if we're in a jubilee parade.
The prayer is drawing to a close
my first term seems a blink away
the school miraging round the bend
me giving Dad a last goodbye;
and now I feel that same dismay
the quiver in my mother's lip
a sudden leap of distancing
as when Odysseus left Penelope
not knowing what to say to her;
or maybe when on leaving Troy
and bound for Ithaca – a home
he'd see afresh with eyes of war –
he put his baffled hands on shoulders
of comrades he'd never see again.

Amen.

Two Rivers Press has been publishing in and about Reading since 1994. Founded by the artist Peter Hay (1951–2003), the press continues to delight readers, local and further afield, with its varied list of individually designed, thought-provoking books.